The Visual Guide to

Asperger's Syndrome in 5-8 Year Olds

by Alis Rowe

Also by Alis Rowe

One Lonely Mind
978-0-9562693-0-0

The Girl with the Curly Hair - Asperger's and Me
978-0-9562693-2-4

The 1st Comic Book
978-0-9562693-1-7

The 2nd Comic Book
978-0-95626934-8

The 3rd Comic Book
978-0-9562693-3-1

The 4th Comic Book
978-15086839-7-1

Websites:
www.thegirlwiththecurlyhair.co.uk

Social Media:
www.facebook.com/thegirlwiththecurlyhair
www.twitter.com/curlyhairedalis

The Visual Guide to

Asperger's Syndrome in 5-8 Year Olds

by Alis Rowe

Lonely Mind Books
London

For parents and teachers of children with Asperger's Syndrome to read with the children

hello

I thought this would be a nice book to get children talking about their difficulties and differences. Use it as a starting point for getting your autistic child to open up and help them realise they're not the only ones who feel the way they do - lots of people, including The Girl with the Curly Hair and The Boy with the Spiky Hair, feel the same way!

Alis aka The Girl with the Curly Hair

Contents

What is autism?

The Girl with the Curly Hair knows what autism is to her...

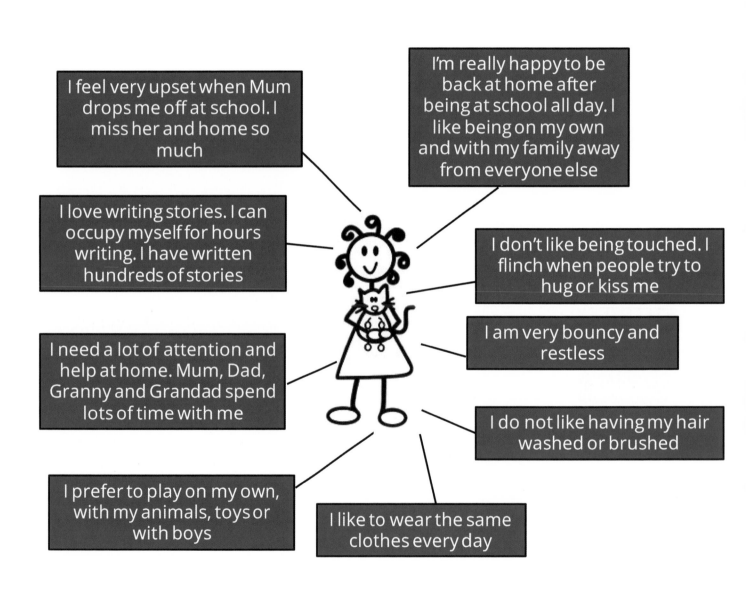

I feel very upset when Mum drops me off at school. I miss her and home so much

I'm really happy to be back at home after being at school all day. I like being on my own and with my family away from everyone else

I love writing stories. I can occupy myself for hours writing. I have written hundreds of stories

I don't like being touched. I flinch when people try to hug or kiss me

I need a lot of attention and help at home. Mum, Dad, Granny and Grandad spend lots of time with me

I am very bouncy and restless

I do not like having my hair washed or brushed

I prefer to play on my own, with my animals, toys or with boys

I like to wear the same clothes every day

The Boy with the Spiky Hair knows what autism is to him...

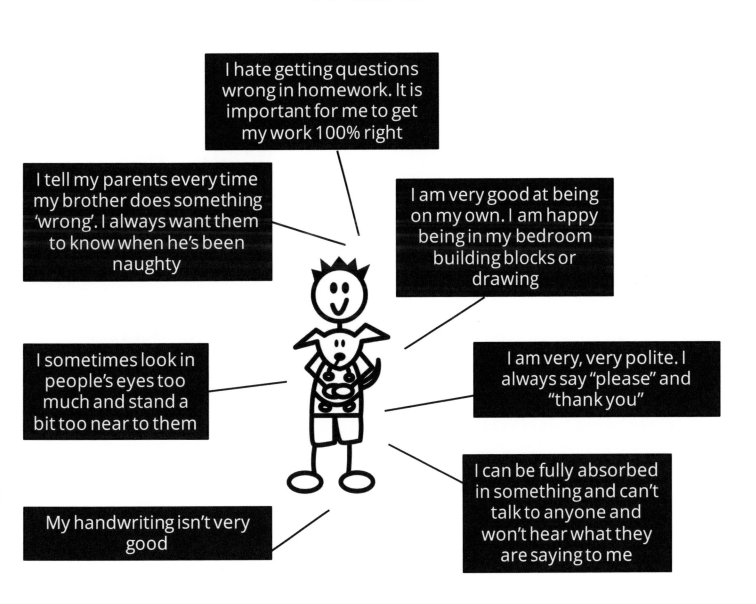

I hate getting questions wrong in homework. It is important for me to get my work 100% right

I tell my parents every time my brother does something 'wrong'. I always want them to know when he's been naughty

I am very good at being on my own. I am happy being in my bedroom building blocks or drawing

I sometimes look in people's eyes too much and stand a bit too near to them

I am very, very polite. I always say "please" and "thank you"

My handwriting isn't very good

I can be fully absorbed in something and can't talk to anyone and won't hear what they are saying to me

The Girl with the Curly Hair says that people like her and The Boy with the Spiky Hair, are a very special sort of people

Most people aren't like them... which means they have unique minds and interesting skills

But it also means they stand out (and sometimes they might not want to)

Do you ever feel 'different' or as though you stand out?

Friendships

The Girl with the Curly Hair tends to get on best with boys. The boys think she's really cool!

The girls think she's a bit weird. The teachers think she ought to have more female friends

The Boy with the Spiky Hair has a few friends, but they sometimes leave him out

Do you have friends?

If you don't, would you like friends?

Do you ever feel left out when you are with others?

Do people pick on you because you aren't like them?

The Girl with the Curly Hair likes writing stories and playing with toy animals

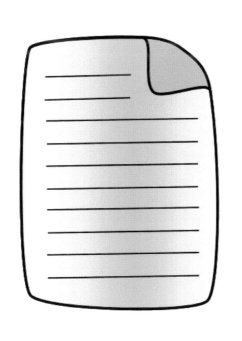

The Boy with the Spiky Hair likes playing with building blocks or reading about and looking at pictures of lifts

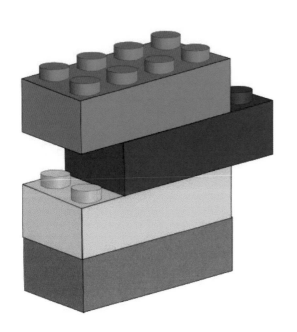

What do you like doing on your own?

Senses

There are at least 5 senses:

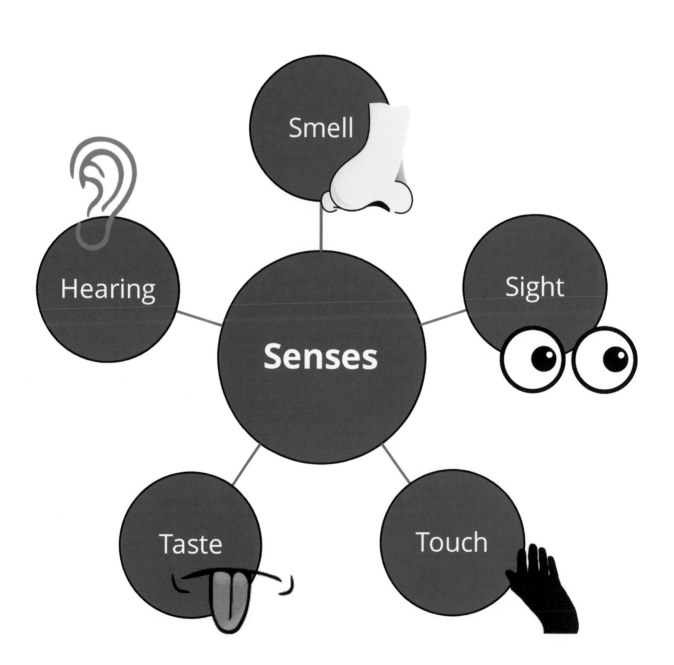

The Girl with the Curly Hair has a very strong sense of smell

She dislikes the smell of B.A.N.A.N.A.S.*

She can smell when Mum or Dad have eaten one, even if it was a long time ago!

They eventually made an agreement that there would be no B.A.N.A.N.A.S. in the house!

The Girl with the Curly Hair hates loud noises – they make her ears hurt. She has to wear earplugs or go out of a room if it is too noisy. She hates motorbikes zooming past

*She doesn't even like to write the word! 27

The Boy with the Spiky Hair has unusual vision

He can see things very clearly that are too far away for others to be able to see

He can notice the fine detail in pictures

Sunlight makes his eyes feel like they are burning, so he has to wear tinted glasses

The Boy with the Spiky Hair loves noise - he always wants the television volume turned up very loudly and he enjoys banging doors and talking loudly

Which of your senses are the strongest and which are the weakest?

What could you do to make your strongest senses a bit more comfortable for you?

Bathing and getting dressed

Why doesn't The Girl with the Curly Hair like having a bath?

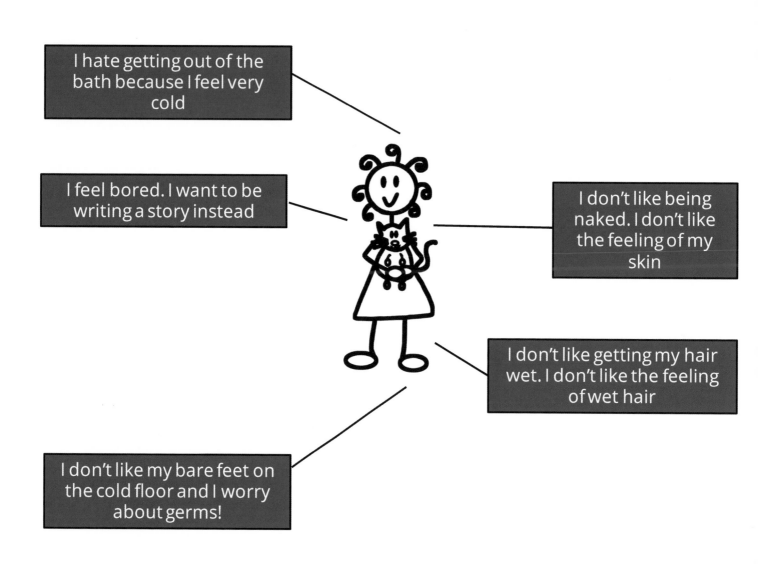

I hate getting out of the bath because I feel very cold

I feel bored. I want to be writing a story instead

I don't like being naked. I don't like the feeling of my skin

I don't like getting my hair wet. I don't like the feeling of wet hair

I don't like my bare feet on the cold floor and I worry about germs!

What makes bath time easier for The Girl with the Curly Hair?

- She always has a bath at the same time every day so she knows to expect it
- She uses a timer so knows exactly how long she has to be in the bath
- She sometimes wears a swimming suit so she doesn't feel naked
- She ties her hair up, wears a bath hat, or keeps the water away from her hair so that it stays dry
- She uses a soft bath mat
- She has a warm towel or warm clothes ready to put on immediately afterwards

What getting dressed is like for The Boy with the Spiky Hair

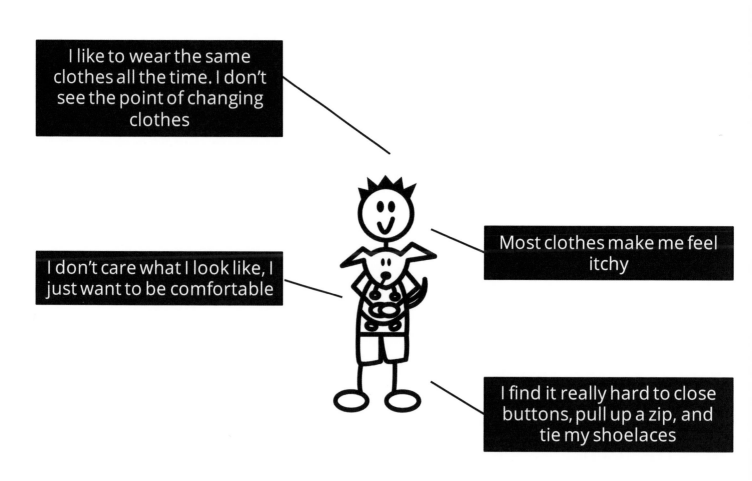

I like to wear the same clothes all the time. I don't see the point of changing clothes

I don't care what I look like, I just want to be comfortable

Most clothes make me feel itchy

I find it really hard to close buttons, pull up a zip, and tie my shoelaces

What makes getting dressed for The Boy with the Spiky Hair easier?

- He wears versatile clothes that are suitable for lots of different occasions such as plain jogging bottoms and a plain T-shirt
- He has clothes with very big buttons and an easy zip to make them easier to close
- He has slip on shoes or shoes with velcro that are easy to take on and off
- When he finds an item of clothing he likes, he gets several to make them last
- He understands that it makes other people happy if he looks 'smart', even if he doesn't care what he looks like
- He cuts the inside labels off because they are itchy

Do you like having a bath? Why do you or why don't you like this?

What makes having a bath more fun?

Do you like getting dressed and wearing stylish clothes? Why do you or why don't you like this?

What makes changing clothes easier?

Food

The Girl with the Curly Hair and The Boy with the Spiky Hair are both fussy eaters

The Girl with the Curly Hair only likes very plain food such as scrambled eggs, peas, bread, corn flakes and cheese & tomato pizza

She doesn't like any extra salt or pepper and really dislikes sauces

She likes to drink from her own glass because if she uses another person's, she can often taste the remains of their orange juice (even if the glass is clean)

The Boy with the Spiky Hair doesn't like different foods touching one another

He will never eat beans *on* toast for example, his Dad has to serve him toast on one plate and beans in a bowl on the side

The Boy with the Spiky Hair loves eating lots of different textured food, such as *crispy* crisps, *wet* cucumber, *hard* nuts, *crunchy* toast, *soft* mashed potato and *chewy* sweets

He will only eat sandwiches if they are cut into *triangles*

What do you like to eat?

Will you only eat certain foods if they are served in a particular way?

Does the temperature, texture and colour of the food matter to you?

Do you prefer just cheese & tomato pizza or a pizza with lots of toppings?

Sleep

The Girl with the Curly Hair and The Boy with the Spiky Hair find it difficult to sleep

They don't like stopping what they are doing to go to bed

The Girl with the Curly Hair doesn't often feel tired

The Boy with the Spiky Hair never wants to stop looking at pictures of lifts in his book. He wants to see them all night long

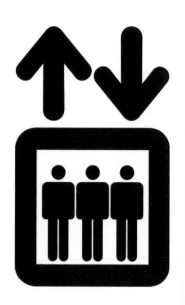

They both feel more sleepy at night if they are more active during the daytime

The Girl with the Curly Hair enjoys skipping, The Boy with the Spiky Hair likes to bounce on his trampoline

What does The Girl with the Curly Hair do to make sleeping easier?

She has blackout blinds (the light keeps her up)

She has a fan on (she likes the noise)

How does The Girl with the Curly Hair make sleeping easier?

She puts lavender oil on her pillow

She has her favourite cuddly bear toy

Mum and Dad massage her shoulders and calf muscles

What does The Boy with the Spiky Hair do to make sleeping easier?

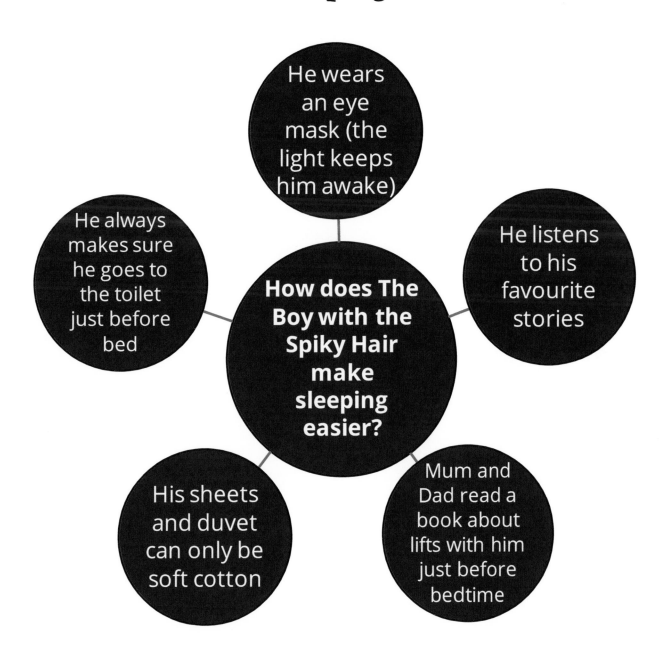

He wears an eye mask (the light keeps him awake)

He always makes sure he goes to the toilet just before bed

How does The Boy with the Spiky Hair make sleeping easier?

He listens to his favourite stories

His sheets and duvet can only be soft cotton

Mum and Dad read a book about lifts with him just before bedtime

Do you find sleeping difficult?

Does the light keep you up, or the noise outside or from the rest of the house?

Does the feel of your sheets and pyjamas against your skin affect how you sleep?

Is there a particular smell you find relaxing that you could put on your pillow?

Do you find it comforting to eat or drink something or use the toilet just before bed?

Social skills

What does The Boy with the Spiky Hair find most difficult about interacting with others?

WHY DO PEOPLE SAY THEY'LL "BE BACK IN 5 MINUTES" IF THEY'RE NOT GOING TO BE?

HOW DO I JUMP INTO A CONVERSATION?

HOW CLOSE DO I STAND TO SOMEONE?

WHEN SHOULD I LOOK IN THEIR EYES?

WHY DON'T PEOPLE LAUGH AT MY JOKES?

WHAT DO THOSE FUNNY PHRASES LIKE "IT'S RAINING CATS AND DOGS" AND "PULL YOUR SOCKS UP" REALLY MEAN?

HOW DO I KNOW WHEN SOMEONE IS TELLING A JOKE?

What does The Girl with the Curly Hair find most difficult about interacting with others?

Do you find talking to people hard too?

Why?

What makes it easier?

Feelings

Both The Boy with the Spiky Hair and The Girl with the Curly Hair find it hard to cope with their feelings

They have very strong feelings and get upset and angry a lot of the time

They often find themselves screaming, shouting and kicking or hitting, or bursting into tears

Sometimes these reactions are because other children do things in the 'wrong' way:

Sometimes these reactions are because what was planned did not go as they expected:

Sometimes these reactions are because moving from one activity to another is hard:

Sometimes these reactions are called 'meltdowns' and can happen because a large amount of *anxiety* has built up over the course of the day

Meltdowns are a bit like a volcano erupting or a bucket overflowing

'bucket' getting more full as the day goes on

The Girl with the Curly Hair has learned to go to her bedroom when she starts to feel angry or upset so that she can calm down. Writing a story helps her deal with her feelings

The Boy with the Spiky Hair has learned to squeeze his shoulders when he starts to feel angry or upset so that he can calm down. He takes deep breaths and goes to his room

Do you get very angry or very upset? What sorts of things make you feel this way?

Do you often feel like your volcano is about to erupt or your bucket might overflow?

What can you do to cool the volcano down or make the bucket less full?

Routines

A routine means doing the same activity regularly or doing a particular activity in a certain way

The Girl with the Curly Hair and The Boy with the Spiky Hair both like having a routine

They feel very upset when their routines get disrupted

The Boy with the Spiky Hair has lots of different routines, such as...

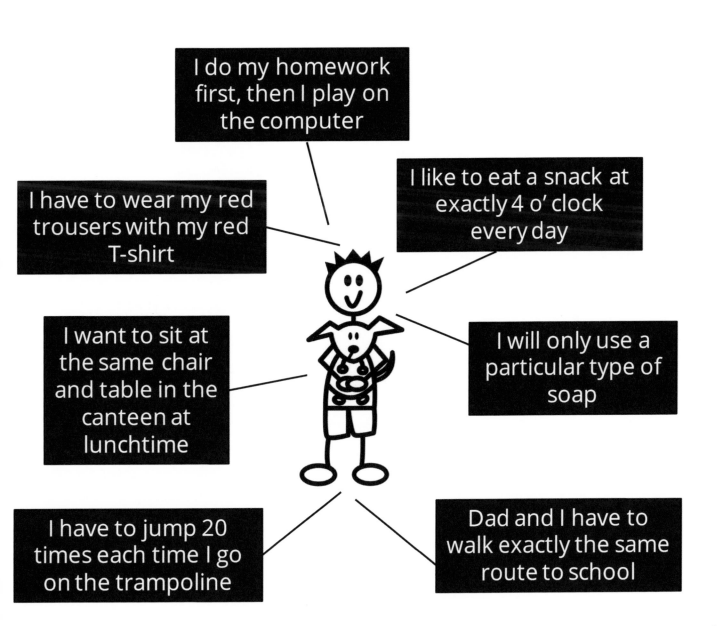

I do my homework first, then I play on the computer

I like to eat a snack at exactly 4 o' clock every day

I have to wear my red trousers with my red T-shirt

I want to sit at the same chair and table in the canteen at lunchtime

I will only use a particular type of soap

I have to jump 20 times each time I go on the trampoline

Dad and I have to walk exactly the same route to school

The Girl with the Curly Hair has lots of different routines, such as...

I only want to drink from my own special mug

I will only eat breakfast after I have got dressed

I always eat eggs on toast for dinner

I have to put my toys in the right place before I go to sleep

I always go to the park at 2 o' clock on Saturday

I don't like being told to stop what I am doing

I want Mum to wait in exactly the same place in the playground every day

Some routines are helpful because they help The Girl with the Curly Hair and The Boy with the Spiky Hair feel happy and relaxed

Some routines are unhelpful because they affect the rest of the family, for example Mum and Dad cancelled going to the park at 2 o' clock on Saturday with The Girl with the Curly Hair because it was raining. They wanted to play a board game instead but The Girl with the Curly Hair got very upset

It would be much better if The Girl with the Curly Hair learned that sometimes activities might have to be changed and that it's OK to do different things instead

There were no more eggs left so Dad made The Girl with the Curly Hair cheese on toast for dinner instead, which made her very upset. It would be much more helpful for The Girl with the Curly Hair to learn that it's OK to eat different things sometimes. Food does occasionally run out – if it does happen we have to cope!

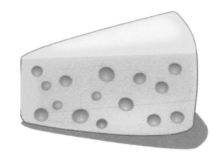

What routines do you have?

Why do you have them?

Are your routines helpful or unhelpful?

How do you feel when your routine gets changed?

How could you better learn to cope when your routine gets changed?

Being organised

Being organised means knowing things like:

- what you're going to be doing tomorrow
- what lessons you have at school today
- what your homework is
- whether you need to bring P.E. kit into school
- knowing what time it is
- what you want to eat for breakfast

The Boy with the Spiky Hair has a lot of trouble with all of these things

Mum and Dad have to use lots of calendars, folders, lists and timers to help him

He always seems to be late to get ready for school

  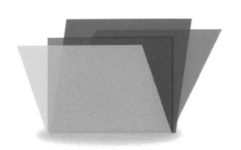 

The Girl with the Curly Hair on the other hand, is very organised

She uses calendars, folders, colour charts, lists and timers but she does all of that by herself!

She always knows what time it is

She's never late for school

How often do you forget your homework?

Do you know what time it is and what you're supposed to be doing right now?

Are you often late for school or are you always on time?

What helps you keep organised?

Summary

There are lots of children on the autistic spectrum a bit like The Girl with the Curly Hair and The Boy with the Spiky Hair

Children have differences and difficulties with friendships, social skills, feelings, senses, routines and keeping organised

This book is a good starting point to talk with your autistic child and for them to tell you about themselves

Many thanks for reading

Other books in The Visual Guides series at the time of writing:

Asperger's Syndrome (1)
Asperger's Syndrome: Meltdowns and Shutdowns
Asperger's Syndrome in 8-11 Year Olds
Asperger's Syndrome in 13-16 Year Olds
Asperger's Syndrome in 16-18 Year Olds
Asperger's Syndrome: Helping Siblings
Asperger's Syndrome and Anxiety
Asperger's Syndrome: Socialising & Social Energy
Asperger's Syndrome and Puberty
Asperger's Syndrome: Meltdowns and Shutdowns (2)
Adapting Health Therapies for People on the Autism Spectrum
Asperger's Syndrome and Emotions
Asperger's Syndrome and Communication
Asperger's Syndrome and Executive Function
Asperger's Syndrome: Understanding Each Other (For ASD/NT Couples)

New titles are continually being produced so keep an eye out!

Printed in Poland
by Amazon Fulfillment
Poland Sp. z o.o., Wrocław